How to ACE your French oral

Questions and answers on all topics

Sample presentation with top phrases to use

Role play tips and examples

With English translation and glossary

This book is dedicated to all my students, past and present. They are too many to list here, but a very special mention goes out to Max Trapnell, future world tennis champion and most importantly an inspiration to everyone who has seen his superb French in action.

TABLE OF CONTENTS

Introduction

In my ten years of tutoring French, I have helped hundreds of students get top marks in their oral exam. In this book I have combined all the questions I have ever seen on a school list and produced a set of answers together with an English translation and glossary of key phrases. One size does not fit all, and you may wish to cut and paste, pick and choose which answers or phrases you include in your own work. You may need to change the description of your family, town and school in order to be factually correct but the overall structures and expressions can still be included.

It's not cheating!

Languages are hard to learn in a classroom, and teachers rarely have enough time to give each student the one-to-one time they need for oral practice. There are plenty of students out there getting help outside school, and here's your chance to be one of them.

Children learn by hearing and copying, and that's what is happening here. Once those phrases are stuck in your head, you'll be able to use them not only in the oral exam but out and about in real life. To make the most of the learning experience, test yourself by looking at the English and translating it into French, then checking with the French text.

There is a fair bit of repetition, and obviously on the day you shouldn't repeat the French for "I'm lucky because" at the beginning of every answer, but I have put them in wherever possible, to show you what is possible, and also because you will only be asked a handful of questions, so you need to make the most of the chance to show off.

There is a positive thread running throughout the answers. If you use them word for word you will end up sounding like a super-hardworking clean-living tennis fiend with a strong environmental awareness and an abundance of energy.

Even if this isn't you, pretending that it is will give you a chance to use some great French idioms. Girls will need to make a few adjustments, as the viewpoint is mainly male so adjectives are masculine and past participles with être are based on the male subject. It's not sexist, or if it is, it's the other way round. More boys than girls struggle with French, I have found.

I have highlighted the structures and expressions examiners will be looking out for, so you'll see how it's possible to change a boring sentence like "I live in London" earning you no points at all, to something much more eye-catching like "I'm lucky because I've been living in London for 5 years and it's the best city in the world."

I have begun the book with a focus on the presentation, which is required in some form by all exam boards, and at the back there is a section on role play which is required by most exam boards, except, notably, Edexcel IGCSE. It's probably only a matter of time!

All these highlighted structures are listed in the glossary, so test yourself on the glossary pages to get an intensive immersion experience in the top phrases.

As I tell my students, fire these highlighted expressions at the examiner like a machine gun, not just in the oral, but in your writing as well, and you'll be well on the way to top marks. So what are you waiting for? Go knock 'em dead!

PART 1

PRESENTATION

NOTES

Your presentation

Depending on your exam board, you may have to either describe a photo you have found yourself, answer questions on a photocard with a few minutes preparation time or make a speech lasting about a minute on one of the set topics.

The photocard is not easy to prepare for, but in the case of the prepapred speeches, make sure you maximise your use of impressive phrases, use all the tenses you can cram in, and leave the examiner to ask boring questions like "what is he / she wearing?"

Here is an example of a description of a picture: this happens to be a cartoon picture of a family on a beach holiday, with a sinister shark fin poking out of the water. In red, you will see the top examiner-pleasing phrases with their translations below. This would be an Edexcel IGCSE full marks answer:

Les vacances

Cette photo a été prise l'année dernière quand nous étions en vacances en Australie. Vous me voyez à gauche, allongée sur une serviette verte, vêtue de bikini, pendant que ma cousine est en train de construire un château de sable. A côté de moi il y a des parasols que l'on peut utiliser pour s'abriter de la chaleur. Tout près, mon père vient de prendre une photo de mon frère qui fait du surf. Il est plus courageux que moi et ma mère semble fière de lui car elle le regarde en souriant. Mais elle veut qu'il fasse attention ! Malheureusement personne n'a aperçu l'aileron du requin qui est sur le point de dévorer la moitié de ma famille. Quel cauchemar ! A l'arrière-plan un jeune homme fait du parapente et lui, comme le pilote du petit avion, aurait eu une vue magnifique de l'attaque de requin. Nous avons tous eu de la chance car il s'est avéré que le requin n'avait pas faim. A part ce presqu'accident, c'étaient des vacances parfaites, un petit coin de paradis et j'ai hâte d'y retourner un jour.

Analysis of key examiner-pleasing expressions

a été prise	This is an expression in the passive voice that literally means *has been taken.*
allongée	Past participle – *stretched out*
vêtue de	Past participle expression – *dressed in* – which is followed by the clothing item without an article (vêtue de bikini)
en train de	In the middle of
que l'on peut utiliser	Relative pronoun *que,* and a modal *peut*
vient de	Has just - from *venir de* (literally *he comes from* taking a photo)
plus courageux que	*Braver than* (superlatives and comparatives win you points)
elle le regarde	She looks at *him* (preceding direct object pronoun)
en souriant	Literally *while smiling*
elle veut qu'il fasse attention	She wants *that he be careful* (note use of subjunctive where instead of *fait* we have *fasse* after an expression of wishing)

personne n'a aperçu	*Personne* (nobody) takes a negative verb
sur le point de	Literally *on the point of*
quel cauchemar !	What a nightmare! This is an exclamation which will always enrich speaking and writing
aurait eu une vue magnifique	Past conditional (use this tense in your presentation as much less easy to use elsewhere
nous avons eu de la chance	We were all lucky (literally *we all had some luck)*
il s'est avéré que	*It turned out that* (this is a very sophisticated expression)
n'avait pas faim	Was not hungry (literally *did not have hunger)* and note the use of the imperfect tense as hungry is a state rather than an event
un petit coin de paradis	An idiom for a delightful location
j'ai hâte d'y retourner	(literally *I have haste to there return)* and this includes not only the idiom for *looking forward* but also the pronoun *y*

Full translation

This photo was taken last year when we were on holiday in Australia. You can see me on the left, lying on a green towel, wearing a bikini, while my cousin is in the middle of building a sand castle. Next to me there are parasols you can use to shelter from the heat. Near me, my father has just taken a photo of my brother who is surfing. He is braver than me and my mother seems proud of him as she is looking at him with a smile. But she wants him to be careful! Unfortunately, nobody has noticed the fin of the shark which is about to devour half my family. What a nightmare! In the background, a young man is parasailing, and he, like the pilot of the small plane, would have had a magnificent view of the shark attack. We were all lucky as it turned out the shark wasn't hungry. Apart from this near miss, this was a perfect holiday in a little corner of paradise and I can't wait to go back there one day.

After talking about a photo, you can expect a specific question relating to a particular person in it : **Que fait-il ? / Que fait-elle ?**
Mon petit cousin qu'on voit au premier plan n'a pas encore appris à nager donc il est sur le point d'aller dans la mer avec une bouée mais il a été distrait par un crabe géant qui se précipite vers le château de sable.
My little cousin who you can see in the foreground has not yet learnt to swim so he's about to go in the see with a rubber ring, but he has been distracted by a giant crab which is hurrying towards the sand castle.

Next, they may ask you about the weather, and some specific questions about various people in the picture, what they are wearing, doing, or saying. This will be followed by questions on what happened before the photo (inviting you to use the past tense), what's going to happen next (inviting the future tense, and questions involving the word *ideal* (inviting the conditional tense).

PAST: Qu'est-ce qui s'est passé avant la photo ?

Be prepared to describe what happened before the photo – taking each person in turn, so you need to know your past tense verbs in the he and the they form:

Sample answer – relating to you
Je me suis réveillée, je me suis levée, je suis descendue, j'ai pris mon petit déjeuner. J'ai pris un croissant, un jus d'orange et des fraises, et après avoir mangé j'ai décidé d'aller à la plage parce qu'il faisait beau et j'avais envie de me bronzer.

I woke up, got up, went downstairs, had my breakfast. I had a croissant, an orange juice and strawberries, and after having eaten I decided to go to the beach and I felt like sunbathing.

Alternative answers relating to other people in the picture
Il / elle s'est réveillé(e) / s'est levé(e) / est descendu(e) / a pris son petit déjeuner et après avoir mangé il / elle a décidé d'aller à la plage car il / elle avait envie de se bronzer.
Ils se sont réveillé(e)s / sont descendu(e)s / ont pris leur petit déjeuner, ont décidé d'aller à la plage car ils / elles avaient envie de se bronzer.

FUTURE : Après la photo
Here you will need your future tense verbs as they relate to you and the others in the picture.

Sample answer – relating to you
Après avoir passé la journée à la plage, je vais retourner à l'hôtel pour prendre une douche. Je ferai une petite sieste avant de descendre au restaurant pour manger. Après avoir manger je vais sortir en boite sans que mes parents ne le sachent et je vais rentrer avant qu'ils se réveillent le lendemain, donc il n'en sauront rien !

After having spent the day at the beach, I will go back to the hotel to take a shower. I will have a little nap before going down to the restaurant to eat. After eating I will go clubbing without my parents knowing and I will get back before they wake up the next day so they won't know anything about it!

CONDITIONAL : les vacances idéales

Here you will need the conditional tense, but start with the imperfect so that you have a nice "if" sentence to start it all off – another box ticked!

Si j'étais riche, j'irais en Espagne mais avec mes amis au lieu de ma famille. On resterait dans un hôtel de luxe près de la plage. J'y irais en avion, première classe, et j'irais à l'hôtel en limousine. Il y aurait tout ce dont j'ai besoin, une piscine, un cinéma, et des courts de tennis réservés pour moi, à l'ombre bien sûr pour éviter la chaleur.

If I was rich I'd go to Spain but with my friends instead of my family. We'd stay in a luxury hotel near the beach. I'd go by plane first class and I'd go to the hotel in a limousine. There would be everything I needed, a pool, a cinema, and tennis courts reserved for me in the shade of course to avoid the heat.

Clothes and accessories

Make sure you know the words for all the clothes items and accessories in the picture, and practise them with the colours, making sure to agree the colour with the gender and number of the item eg.

elle porte une chemise vert**e**
il porte des lunettes blan**ches**
ils portent des chaussures noir**es**

Weather

Il fait assez beau. Il y a quelques nuages mais le soleil brille. On dirait qu'il y a du vent parce qu'il y a des vagues énormes.

It is quite sunny. There are a few clouds but the sun is shining. It looks windy because there are enormous waves.

PART 2

SAMPLE ORAL ANSWERS

NOTES

Top tips for the conversation

- **The examiner wants you to succeed** – so don't imagine that they are trying to trip you up. It is likely to be your own teacher testing you and he or she will want you to get the best result possible.

- **Listen for key words** such as

  idéal (inviting the conditional)

  jeune (when you were younger, so imperfect)

  le weekend dernier (inviting passe compose)

  le weekend prochain (inviting future)

  changer (what you'd like to change, so begin by saying what you don't like)

  tu préfères (you will need to compare two things)

- **They are looking to tick boxes.** The recording will be sent off to moderators and needs to show your mastery of all the main tenses and a good knowledge of the language overall. So if you keep getting asked the same type of question, then chances are you have not yet successfully demonstrated your knowledge of a particular tense.

- **Keep talking!** Stay on topic, but the more you speak the fewer questions will be asked, and the longer you are in control.

- **Take your time** before answering, and remember you can ask the examiner to repeat a question.

- **Don't panic**. It will be over in a few minutes. Smile, breathe and enjoy!

HOME AND ABROAD

Describe your town

J'habite à Wimbledon dans le sud-ouest de Londres, près de Kingston. C'est une ville moderne avec des endroits historiques. J'ai de la chance parce qu'à mon avis c'est la meilleure région de Londres et j'y habite depuis ma naissance. Ce que j'aime c'est qu'il y a tout ce dont j'ai besoin et je ne m'ennuie jamais. On peut aller au cinéma, faire du shopping ou jouer au tennis au parc. Mais, ce que je n'aime pas c'est la circulation – parfois il me faut une demie heure pour aller en ville en bus. S'il y avait plus de pistes cyclables j'irais à vélo mais il n'y en a pas assez donc c'est trop dangereux.

I live in Wimbledon in south-west London near Kingston. It's a modern town with some older parts. I'm lucky because in my opinion it's the best part of London and I've lived there since I was born. What I like is that there is everything I need and I never get bored. You can go to the cinema, go shopping or play tennis in the park; but what I don't like is the traffic. Sometimes it takes me half an hour to get into town on the bus. If there were more cycle paths I'd go by bike but there aren't enough so it's too dangerous.

Describe a recent activity in your town

Le weekend dernier je suis allé en ville avec ma sœur pour acheter un cadeau pour l'anniversaire de ma mère. Je lui ai acheté un livre car elle adore la lecture. Après ça, nous sommes allés au cinéma pour regarder un film de James Bond, que j'ai beaucoup aimé car il y avait de bons effets spéciaux. Ensuite, nous sommes allées au café pour manger un sandwich. Après avoir mangé, nous sommes rentrés chez nous en bus.

Last weekend I went into town with my sister to buy a present for my mother's birthday. I bought her a book as she loves reading. After that we went to the cinema to see a James Bond film which I loved because there were great special effects. Then we went to the café for a sandwich. After eating we went home by bus.

What is there for young people in your town?

Il n'y a pas grand-chose pour les jeunes, il faut l'admettre. On peut aller au cinéma ou à la piscine, on peut faire du shopping ou du bowling, mais tout ça coute cher et la plupart des jeunes n'ont pas les moyens. Ce qu'il manque c'est un endroit où on peut retrouver ses amis quand il fait mauvais, comme un club de jeunesse. S'il y en avait un, on serait tous ravis. A part ça, je pense qu'il devrait y avoir plus de pistes cyclables pour qu'on puisse aller partout à vélo. Ainsi, on pourrait non seulement rester en forme mais aussi réduire la pollution de l'air et protéger l'environnement.

There isn't much for young people I must admit. You can go to the cinema or the pool, go shopping or bowling but all that costs money and most young people can't afford it. What's missing is a place you can meet up with friends when the weather is bad like a youth club. If there was one we would all be so happy. Apart from that I think there should be more cycle paths so we can go everywhere by bike. That way we could not only keep fit but reduce air pollution and protect the environment.

What would you do to improve your town?

Si j'avais l'occasion d'améliorer ma ville, je ferais quelque chose pour les jeunes, parce qu'il n'y a pas grand-chose en ce moment. On peut aller au cinéma ou à la piscine, on peut faire du shopping ou du bowling, mais tout ça coute cher et la plupart des jeunes n'ont pas les moyens. Ce qu'il manque c'est un endroit où on peut retrouver ses amis quand il fait mauvais, comme un club de jeunesse. S'il y en avait un, on serait tous ravis. A part ça, je pense qu'il devrait y avoir plus de pistes cyclables pour qu'on puisse aller partout à vélo. Ainsi, on pourrait non seulement rester en forme mais aussi réduire la pollution de l'air et protéger l'environnement.

If I had the chance to improve my town, I would do something for the young people. You can go to the cinema or the pool, go shopping or bowling but all that costs money and most young people can't afford it. What's missing is a place you can meet up with friends when the weather is bad like a youth club. If there was one we would all be so happy. Apart from that I think there should be more cycle paths so we can go everywhere by bike. That way we could not only keep fit but reduce air pollution and protect the environment.

What is there for tourists in your town?

Pour les touristes, on est super-bien situé pour aller au championnat de tennis, et on peut facilement aller à Londres en train pour visiter les sites touristiques comme le palais de Buckingham et la Tour de Londres, aussi bien que les musées et les galléries d'art. Au centre de Londres il y a plein de théâtres où on peut voir des spectacles mondialement célèbres, mais les billets coutent les yeux de la tête.

For the tourists, we are perfectly placed for the tennis championships and you can get to London easily by train to see the tourist attractions like Buckingham Palace and the Tower of London as well as the museums and art galleries. In the centre of London there are lots o theatres where you can see world famous shows, but the tickets cost an arm and a leg.

Advantages of living in a town

L'avantage d'habiter en ville c'est qu'il y a tout ce dont j'ai besoin et plein de choses à faire. En plus je peux facilement retrouver mes amis en utilisant les transports en commun. Je trouve les bus indispensables. Je m'en sers tous les jours et je ne pourrais pas m'en passer.

The advantage of living in town is that there is everything I need and lots of things to do. Also I can easily meet up with my friends using public transport. I find the buses essential. I use them every day and couldn't manage without them.

Disadvantages of living in a town

Ce que je n'aime pas tellement c'est la pollution de l'air causée par les gaz d'echappement. La pollution provoque le réchauffement de la terre et l'effet de serre mais il me semble que les gens sont trop égoïstes pour abandonner le confort de leurs voitures et prendre le bus. En plus, il n'y a pas assez de pistes cyclables. S'il y en avait plus, j'irais partout à vélo.

What I don't like so much is the air pollution caused by car emissions. Pollution causes global warming and the greenhouse effect but it seems that people are too selfish to abandon the comfort of their cars and take the bus. Also, there aren't enough cycle paths. If there were more, I'd go everywhere by bike.

Advantages of the countryside

A la campagne c'est moins pollué qu'en ville et il y a plus d'espaces verts où on peut se promener et respirer l'air frais. Les prix immobiliers sont plus bas car le terrain coute moins cher. Il y a beaucoup moins de circulation, donc on peut faire du vélo sans avoir peur d'être écrasé par un bus.

In the countryside it's less polluted than in the town and there are more green spaces where you can walk and breathe fresh air. The house prices are lower as land is cheaper. There is a lot less traffic so you can cycle without worrying about being run over by a bus.

Disadvantages of the countryside

A la campagne, bien que ce soit plus tranquille et plus calme, il n'y a rien à faire et on doit aller partout en voiture car il n'y a pas de transports en commun. Je ne voudrais jamais y habiter car je me sentirais trop isolé.

In the countryside, although it's quieter and calmer, there isn't anything to do and you have to go everywhere by car as there is no public transport. I would never want to live there as I'd feel too isolated.

Weather in your region today

Aujourd'hui il fait assez beau mais le ciel est couvert et il va pleuvoir des grenouilles, j'en suis sûr.

Today the weather is quite good but it's cloudy and it's going to pour with rain I'm sure.

Seasonal changes

Normalement en hiver il fait un froid de canard, en été il fait chaud, et au printemps et en automne c'est entre les deux. Du coup, en hiver je fais moins de sport, et je joue au tennis à l'intérieur quand il pleut. Par contre, en été je suis dehors tous les jours. Je passe tout mon temps libre à jouer au tennis et à faire du vélo, car ça fait du bien d'être en plein air et c'est bon pour la santé.

Normally in winter it's freezing cold, in summer it's hot and in the spring and autumn it's between the two. So in winter I do less sport and I play tennis indoors when it's raining. But in summer I'm outside every day. I spend all my free time playing tennis and going cycling, because it feels good to be out in the fresh air and it's good for you.

Climate comparison – England and France

Il n'y a pas beaucoup de différence entre le climat en Angleterre et en France. Mais au sud de la France il fait plus chaud qu'en Angleterre. Plus on va vers le sud, plus la température augmente. C'est le contraire au nord de l'Angleterre – plus on va vers le nord, plus le temps s'empire.

There isn't much difference between the climate in England and France. But in the south of France it's hotter than in England. The further you go southwards, the hotter it gets. It's the opposite in the north of England – the further north you go, the worse the weather gets.

Climate change

Le climat est en train de changer, il n'y a aucun doute. Il ne neige plus en hiver, tandis que pendant les années quatre-vingt il neigeait souvent. Le réchauffement de la terre a déjà causé l'augmentation du niveau des océans et il y a des iles qui commencent à disparaitre. En plus il y a de plus en plus d'ouragans et de tempêtes. Je trouve tout ça effrayant, car il me semble que c'est en cherchant une meilleure vie que nous détruisons notre planète.

There is no doubt that climate change is happening. It doesn't snow anymore in winter, whereas in the 80s it snowed a lot. Global warming has already caused ocean levels to rise and some islands are disappearing. Also there are more and more hurricanes and storms. I find all that frightening, as it seems to me that it is in searching for a better life that we are destroying our planet.

Climate change solution

Il faut qu'on fasse des efforts pour changer nos habitudes, consommer moins, voyager moins, gaspiller moins d'énergie et utiliser l'énergie renouvelable comme l'énergie solaire et éolienne. On devrait utiliser les transports en commun, recycler plus et construire plus de pistes cyclables pour encourager les gens à abandonner leurs voitures.

We've got to make an effort to change our habits, consume less, travel less, waste less energy and use renewable energy like solar and wind power. We should be using public transport, doing more recycling and building more cycle paths to encourage people to leave their cars at home.

Transport in your region

Puisque j'habite à Londres, il y a tous les moyens de transport dont on pourrait avoir besoin – et comme c'est une très grande ville c'est bien de pouvoir se déplacer facilement

On peut prendre le bus, le train, le métro, le tramway et les vélos municipaux qui se trouvent partout. Il suffit de s'enregistrer et on peut prendre un vélo et le déposer ailleurs. Moi je m'en sers tous les jours, pour aller au collège, chez des amis, en ville, quoi que ce soit.

Since I live in London, there are all the modes of transport you could possibly need – and as it's a very big city it's good to be able to move around easily. You can take the bus, train, underground, tram and community bikes which are everywhere. You just have to register and you can take a bike and drop it off elsewhere. I use them every day to go to school to friends' houses, into town, whatever.

Favourite transport

Mon moyen de transport préféré c'est le bus, parce que je m'installe en avant, en haut, et je vois tout qui se passe autour de moi. En plus j'adore faire du vélo. Ce que je n'aime pas, pourtant, c'est le manque de pistes cyclables. On devrait en construire plus pour que les gens puissent se déplacer sans causer la pollution de l'air. Je suis accro au cyclisme et je trouve que c'est un passe-temps dangereux en ville.

My favourite mode of transport is the bus because I sit at the front on top and I see everything that's going on around me. I also love cycling. What I don't like however is the lack of cycle paths. We need to build more so that people can get around without causing air pollution. I'm a cycling addict and I find that it's a dangerous hobby in town.

French-speaking countries you've been to

Je suis allé en France plusieurs fois et je l'ai beaucoup aimée, car le paysage est pittoresque et la cuisine la meilleure du monde. En plus, le climat et plus agréable qu'en Angleterre.

Quant aux autres pays francophones, j'en connais, mais je ne les ai pas visités. On parle français aux iles caraïbes et en Afrique du nord, mais je n'y suis jamais allé.

I've been to France many times and I liked it a lot, as the scenery is picturesque and the food the best in the world. Also the weather is better than in England. As for other French speaking countries, I know some but I haven't been to any. They speak French in the Caribbean and in North Africa but I've never been there.

Usual holidays

J'ai de la chance car nous passons la plupart des vacances en Espagne. J'y vais chaque année en avion avec ma famille. Il y a beaucoup de choses à faire, comme la natation, l'équitation, et la voile. Moi, je passe tout mon temps à jouer au tennis. J'y joue tout le temps, j'y suis accro, je ne pourrais pas m'en passer. J'aime l'Espagne parce qu'il fait beau tout le temps et ne pleut que rarement.

I'm lucky because we spend most of the holidays in Spain. I go there every year by plane with my family. There are lots of things to do like swimming, horse-riding and sailing. I spend all my time playing tennis. I play it all the time, I'm addicted, I couldn't manage without it. I like Spain because the weather is good all the time and it only rarely rains.

Last year's holiday

L'année dernière je suis allé en France en avion avec mes parents. Nous sommes restés dans un hôtel de cinq étoiles au bord de la mer. On a eu de la chance car il faisait beau tous les jours, donc on a pu passer la plupart du temps en plein air. Nous sommes allés à la plage où j'ai appris à faire de la planche à voile et on a goûté les plats régionaux qui étaient délicieux. Nous avons visité des sites touristiques et j'ai pris des photos pour montrer à mes copains. C'était super-chouette. J'ai hâte d'y retourner.

Last year I went to France by plane with my parents. We stayed in a five star hotel at the seaside. We were lucky because the weather was good every day so we were able to spend most of the time in the fresh air. We went to the beach where I learnt to windsurf and we tasted the local dishes which were delicious. We visited tourist attractions and I took pictures to show my friends. It was great. I can't wait to go back there.

Purchases on holiday
En Espagne j'ai acheté un t-shirt pour mon ami avec un taureau dessus parce que c'est l'animal national de l'Espagne. Il l'a adoré. Quand je suis allé en France j'ai rapporté du confit de canard car c'était le plat typique de la région et on ne peut pas le trouver dans les supermarchés anglais.

In Spain I bought a Tshirt for my friend with a bull on it because it's the national animal of Spain. He loved it. When I went to France I brought back confit de canard because it was the local speciality and you can't find it in the English supermarkets.

Future holiday
Cette année j'irai en Italie avec ma famille en avion, pour quinze jours. Nous allons rester dans un hôtel près de la plage où on peut faire de la planche à voile et de la natation. J'en profiterai pour me détendre après mes examens car j'aurai besoin de repos. Je n'en ferai pas une rame. J'espère qu'il fera beau pour que je puisse passer tout mon temps dehors.

This year I'm going to go to Italy with my family by plane for a fortnight. We will stay in a hotel near the beach where you canl go windsurfing and swimming. I'll make the most of it to relax after my exams as I'll be in need of a rest. I won't lift a finger. I hope that the weather will be good so I can spend all my time outside.

Ideal holiday

Si j'étais riche, j'irais en Espagne mais avec mes amis au lieu de ma famille. On resterait dans un hôtel de luxe près de la plage. J'y irais en avion, première classe, et j'irais à l'hôtel en limousine. Je jouerais au tennis tous les jours avec les meilleurs entraineurs du monde pour que je puisse devenir champion du monde. Il y aurait tout ce dont j'ai besoin, une piscine, un cinéma, et des courts de tennis réservés pour moi, à l'ombre bien sûr pour éviter la chaleur.

If I was rich I'd go to Spain but with my friends instead of my family. We'd stay in a luxury hotel near the beach. I'd go by plane first class and I'd go to the hotel in a limousine. I'd play tennis every day with the best trainers in the country so that I could become world champion. There would be everything I needed, a pool, a cinema, and tennis courts reserved for me in the shade of course to avoid the heat.

Holidays with parents v holidays with friends

Si on part en vacances avec les parents, c'est facile et c'est gratuit. Ils paient tout et on ne doit penser à rien. Cependant, c'est eux qui décident ce qui est permis, et on n'a pas beaucoup de choix. Ils me trainent aux musées les plus ennuyeux du monde et j'en ai marre. Avec les amis, on peut s'amuser beaucoup plus, on peut sortir quand on veut, rentrer quand on veut et manger ce qu'on veut. J'ai hâte de partir avec mes copains dès que j'aurai l'occasion.

If you go on holiday with parents it's easy and free. They pay for everything and you don't need to think about anything. However, they are the ones that decide what is allowed and you don't get much choice. They drag me round the most boring museums in the world and I'm sick of it. With friends you can have much more fun, you can go out when you like, come back when you like and eat what you like. I can't wait to go away with my friends as soon as I get the chance.

Essential ingredients of a holiday

Pour moi ce qui est important c'est le climat. Il faut que le temps soit ensoleillé mais je n'aime pas une chaleur insupportable. En plus, j'aimerais avoir mes amis avec moi, car on s'amuse tellement bien ensemble. Aussi, il faut loger dans un hôtel de luxe pour pouvoir se détendre et oublier le stress de la vie à Londres.

For me what's important is the climate. The weather has to be sunny but I don't like unbearable heat. Also I'd like to have my friends with me, as we have so much fun together. And we'd have to be in a luxury hotel in order to be able to relax and forget the stress of London life.

Importance of holidays generally

Bien que j'adore ma maison et mon quartier, je trouve que les vacances sont essentielles pour beaucoup de raisons. On peut se détendre après avoir travaillé pendant des mois. On peut explorer de nouveaux pays et connaitre de nouvelles cultures. On peut essayer de nouvelles activités et gouter la cuisine régionale. Mais ce que je trouve le plus important c'est passer du temps avec ma famille, car normalement on ne se voit pas assez souvent.

Although I love my house and my area, I find that holidays are essential for many reasons. You can relax after working for months. You can explore new countries and get to know new cultures. You can try out new activities and taste the local dishes. But what I find most important is spending time with my family as normally we don't see each other often enough.

Camping

Je n'ai jamais fait de camping, mais j'ai envie de l'essayer car ça me parait super-amusant de vivre en plein air dans une tente. Cependant, je ne voudrais pas tellement dormir parterre sans matelas. Ça doit faire mal, non?

I've never been camping but I'd like to try it as it seems really fun to live outdoors in a tent. However I wouldn't really like to sleep on the floor without a mattress. That must hurt surely!

Festivals in England

Il n'y a pas beaucoup de festivals en Angleterre. Le seul festival qu'on fête normalement chez moi c'est noël. J'adore noël, car j'ai l'occasion de passer du temps avec ma famille, y compris les cousins que je ne vois qu'une fois par an. On mange un repas splendide et après avoir regardé le discours de la reine à la télé, on joue aux jeux de société ensemble et on échange des cadeaux. Ça fait du bien, passer du temps en famille.

There aren't many festivals in England. The only one that we normally celebrate in my family is Christmas. I love Christmas as I have the chance to spend time with my family, including the cousins that I only see once a year. We eat an amazing meal and after watching the Queen's speech we play board games together and exchange presents. It feels good spending time with family.

Last Christmas

L'année dernière toute ma famille est venue chez nous, y compris mes cousins que je ne vois qu'une fois par an. On a mangé un repas splendide, et après avoir regardé le discours de la reine à la télé on a joué aux jeux de société ensemble et on a échangé des cadeaux. J'ai offert une peinture à ma grand-mère et elle en était ravie. Moi j'ai reçu des vêtements et des nouveaux baskets dont j'avais rêvé depuis longtemps. C'était super.

Last year all my family came to us including my cousins whom I only see once a year. We ate an amazing meal and after watching the Queen's speech we played board games together and exchanged presents. I gave a painting to my granny and she was delighted. I received clothes and new trainers I'd been dreaming about for ages. It was great.

Importance of festivals

Les festivals sont importants car on n'a pas souvent l'occasion de passer du temps en famille et ça fait du bien. En Angleterre c'est dommage parce qu'on accorde de moins en moins d'importance à la religion, et c'est en abandonnant la religion qu'on perd les fêtes. En Espagne par exemple, il y a la fête de Pâques qui dure une semaine tandis que chez moi ce n'est que deux jours fériés pleins de chocolat.

Festivals are important because we don't often get the chance to spend time together as a family and it feels good. In England it's a shame because religion has become less and less important and it's in abandoning religion that we lose our festivals. In Spain for example there is the festival of Easter that lasts a week whereas here it's just two bank holidays full of chocolate.

EDUCATION AND WORK

Describe your school

Mon collège s'appelle …………. et se trouve à ………………., près de Londres. J'ai de la chance parce que c'est le meilleur collège du monde et j'y vais depuis cinq ans. C'est un collège pour les garçons, c'est grand, ancien, et bien équipé. Il y a environ mille élèves. Il y a des salles de classe, des terrains de sport où on peut jouer au foot, des laboratoires, une bibliothèque et une cantine.

My school is called ……………. and it is in …………………………. near London. I'm lucky because it's the best school in the world and I've been going there for five years. It's a boys' school, it's big, old and well equipped. There are about a thousand students. There are classrooms, sports fields where you can play football, laboratories, a library and a canteen.

Likes and dislikes at school

Ce que j'aime c'est que j'ai beaucoup d'amis, les profs sont sympas et on peut faire beaucoup de sport. Ce que je n'aime pas c'est que les profs nous donnent trop de devoirs, on doit porter un uniforme et les règles sont strictes – par exemple on ne peut pas parler en classe, et on ne peut pas utiliser les portables.

What I like is that I have lots of friends, the teachers are nice and you can do a lot of sport. What I don't like is that the teachers give us too much homework. Also, we have to wear a uniform and the rules are strict – for example we can't talk in class and we can't use mobile phones.

The school day

La journée scolaire commence à huit heures et termine à quatre heures. Je suis obligé de me lever à sept heures et demie pour que je puisse arriver au collège à l'heure. J'ai de la chance car j'habite tout près de mon collège, donc j'y vais à pied et parfois j'arrive de bonne heure et j'en profite pour terminer mes devoirs et envoyer des textos. Dès que j'arrive au collège, je retrouve mes amis et on bavarde avant que les cours commencent à 9h. Il y a huit cours par jour et chaque cours dure 45 minutes. La pause déjeuner est à 1h. Pendant la pause je mange un sandwich et je joue au foot avec mes amis. Les cours finissent à 4h et je rentre chez moi, mais je ne peux me relaxer qu'après avoir fait mes devoirs.

My school day begins at 8am and finishes at 4pm. I have to get up at 7am so I can get to school on time. I'm lucky because I live very near my school so I go there on foot and sometimes I get there early and make the most of it to finish my homework and send some texts. As soon as I arrive at school I meet my friends and chat before lessons begin at 9. There are 8 lessons a day and each lesson lasts 45 minutes. The lunch hour is at 1. During the break I eat a sandwich and play football with my friends. Lessons finish at 4 and I go home but I can't relax until I've done my homework.

Favourite subjects

Ma matière préférée c'est le français parce que j'ai de bonnes notes, je le trouve facile et le prof est sympa. Je n'aime pas le latin parce que je le trouve ennuyeux, le prof est nul et il nous donne trop de devoirs. Aussi, j'étudie les maths, les sciences, l'anglais, le sport, le dessin, la musique, la géo et l'histoire.

My favourite subject is French because I get good marks, I find it easy and the teacher is nice. I don't like Latin because I find it boring, the teacher is rubbish and gives us too much homework. I also do maths, science, English, sport, art, music, geography and history.

Describe a teacher

Mon prof préféré c'est Monsieur Macpherson, mon prof d'histoire. Il est super-sympa et marrant et ne nous donne pas trop de devoirs. Cependant il est très intelligent et il n'y a rien qu'il ne sait pas. Je l'admire pour ça, car j'aimerais être aussi intelligent que lui.

My favourite teacher is Mr Macpherson my history teacher. He is really nice and funny and doesn't give too much homework. However, he is very clever and there's nothing he doesn't know. I admire him for that, as I'd like to be as clever as him.

Describe school uniform

A mon école on doit porter un uniforme. Je porte un pantalon noir, une chemise blanche, des chaussures noires, des chaussettes noires, une cravate et une veste.

At my school we have to wear a uniform. I wear black trousers, a white shirt, black shoes, black socks, a tie and a jacket.

Opinion of school uniform

Bien que l'uniforme soit utile pour encourager la discipline, je trouve qu'on ne peut pas montrer son individualité quand tout le monde se ressemble. J'aurais peut-être du mal au début si je devais penser à mes vêtements tous les jours, mais cela dit, J'aimerais mieux imiter le système français et m'habiller comme je veux.

Although uniform is useful to encourage discipline, I find that you can't show your individuality when everyone looks the same. I might find it hard at first if I had to think about my clothes every day but having said that, I would rather do as the French do and wear what I like.

Yesterday at school

Hier j'ai eu une journée parfaite. Je suis arrivé au collège à huit heures et après avoir mis mes affaires dans mon casier, j'ai pris mes cahiers et mes livres pour les deux premiers cours. Puis je suis allé à ma salle de classe et j'ai bavardé avec mes amis. Le prof de maths a annulé notre contrôle et le prof d'anglais était absent. Pendant la pause déjeuner mes copains et moi sommes allés au terrain de sport pour jouer au foot. L'après-midi il n'y avait que deux cours de plus car j'ai dû participer au concours de tennis et heureusement j'ai gagné !

Yesterday I had a perfect day. I arrived at school at 8 and after putting my things in my locker I took my books for the first two lessons. Then I went to my classroom and chatted with my friends. The maths teacher cancelled our test and the English teacher was away. During lunch my friends and I went to the sports field to play football. In the afternoon there were only two more lessons as I had to play in a tennis competition and luckily I won!

Homework

Normalement je fais mes devoirs dans la cuisine, mais hier soir j'ai dû faire mes devoirs de maths et de français dans ma chambre parce qu'on avait des invités. Je trouve les devoirs utiles pour pratiquer ce qu'on a appris en classe, mais si j'étais prof je ne les donnerais pas chaque semaine. Parfois on devrait avoir le droit de se détendre un peu.

Normally I do my homework in the kitchen but last night I had to do my French and maths homework in my bedroom because we had visitors. I find homework useful to practice what we have learnt in class, but if I was a teacher I wouldn't give it every week. Sometimes we should be able to relax a bit.

School trips

Hier, j'ai eu de la chance car moi et mes amis sommes allées à Londres pour assister à un concert au Festival Hall. C'était un voyage scolaire avec tous mes copains qui étudient la musique. La musique était extraordinaire et je l'ai adoré. Je suis rentré très tard chez moi et le lendemain j'étais très fatiguée. J'ai envie d'y retourner parce que ça m'a vraiment inspiré.

Yesterday I was lucky because my friends and I went to London to see a concert at the Festival Hall. It was a school trip with all my friends who study music. The music was extraordinary and I loved it. I got home very late and the next day I was very tired. I would like to go back there because it really inspired me.

Clubs after school

A mon collège on peut faire de la natation, jouer au foot ou au badminton et il y a des clubs d'échecs, de foot et de lecture. J'ai de la chance parce que je ne m'ennuie jamais. Moi je fais de l'aviron le samedi et je joue au tennis pour mon équipe scolaire.

At my school you can do swimming, play football or badminton and there are chess, football and reading clubs. I'm lucky because I never get bored. I do rowing on a Saturday and I play tennis for my school team.

Ideal school

Mon collège idéal serait grand, moderne, tout près de chez moi pour que je puisse y aller à pied. Il y aurait une énorme piscine et un cinéma. Les cours commenceraient à midi et termineraient à quinze heures. Il n'y aurait pas d'uniforme et on ne serait pas obligé d'aller au cours de maths.

My ideal school would be big, modern and very near my home so I could go there on foot. There would be an enormous swimming pool and a cinema. Lessons would begin at midday and would finish at 3pm. There would be no uniform and we wouldn't have to go to maths lessons.

What you'd change if you could

Si je pouvais changer quelque chose, je changerais l'uniforme car c'est ennuyeux de porter la même chose tous les jours. Je voudrais plutôt porter un jean et un pull. En plus, je changerais l'horaire scolaire et l'emploi de temps, parce que les scientifiques ont prouvé que les ados ont besoin de plus de sommeil le matin. Si je pouvais commencer et terminer plus tard, je pourrais me concentrer mieux et j'aurais de meilleures notes.

If I could change something I would change the uniform as it's boring wearing the same thing every day. I'd rather wear jeans and a jumper. Also I would change the school timetable because scientists have proved that teenagers need more sleep in the mornings. If I could start and finish later I would be able to concentrate better and I would get better grades.

Primary school

Quand j'étais plus jeune j'allais à une école primaire qui s'appelle ………….. C'était petit, mais plus amical et plus sympa que mon nouveau collège car il n'y avait pas beaucoup de devoirs et on n'était pas obligé de porter un uniforme.

When I was younger I went to a primary school called……………. It was small but more friendly and nicer than my new school as there wasn't much homework and we didn't have to wear a uniform.

Future education

Pour le bac, j'étudierai la géographie, la philosophie et l'économie parce que ce sont mes matières préférées et j'ai de bonnes notes. En plus, les profs sont sympas donc j'espère qu'ils ne nous donneront pas trop de devoirs. Je devrai travailler dur pendant les deux ans, bien que ce soit ennuyeux, pour que je puisse continuer mes études à l'université. Je voudrais aller à l'université d'Oxford pour étudier l'économie. Apres avoir fini mes études, il faudra que je trouve un emploi où je peux gagner un énorme salaire, afin de pouvoir prendre la retraite à trente-cinq ans.

For my A levels I will study geography, philosoophy and economics because they are my favourite subjects and I get good grades. Also the teachers are nice so I I hope they won't give me too much homework. I will have to work hard over the two years although it's boring, so that I can continue my studies at university. I'd like to go to Oxford University to study economics. When I've finished studying I'll have to find a job where I can earn an enormous salary in order to be able to retire at 35.

Part time job

Je n'ai pas de boulot en ce moment car je n'ai pas le temps – les profs nous donnent trop de devoirs et je passe tout mon temps libre à jouer au tennis.

I haven't got a job as I don't have the time – the teachers give us too much homework and I spend all my free time playing tennis.

Work experience

Je n'ai pas encore fait de stage en entreprise car je n'ai que seize ans, mais j'ai envie d'avoir l'occasion de travailler dans un cabinet juridique pour savoir si j'aimerais ce genre de boulot à l'avenir. C'est important que les jeunes aient de l'expérience du monde de travail pour qu'ils puissent se rendre compte de ce que font les adultes tous les jours.

I have not yet done any work experience as I am only 16, but I would like to have the chance to work in a law firm to see if I would like that kind of job in the future. It's important that young people have experience of the world of work so that they realise what adults do every day.

Future job

Je ne sais pas encore ce que je vais faire mais il faut que ce soit intéressant et passionnant. Avant tout je voudrais gagner tous les tournois de tennis et être champion du monde. Sinon, j'aimerais être prof pour que je puisse profiter des longues vacances ! Et je voudrais travailler avec les jeunes car c'est plus enrichissant que bosser dans un bureau.

I don't know yet what I'm going to do but it's got to be interesting and exciting. Above all I would like to win all the tennis tournaments and be world champion. Otherwise I'd like to be a teacher so I can make the most of the long holidays, and I'd like to work with young people because it's more gratifying than working in an office.

Ideal job

Je voudrais bien travailler à l'étranger pour que je puisse pratiquer mon français et mon espagnol. Après avoir étudié pendant autant d'années ce serait dommage de tout abandonner. En plus, si je suis champion de tennis je vais devoir voyager! Mon emploi idéal serait joueur de tennis professionnel – c'est mon rêve tout simplement.

A mon avis c'est important de suivre ses rêves, même si on ne réussit pas. Il faut au moins qu'on essaie.

I would like to work abroad so I could practise my French and Spanish. After studying for so many years it would be a shame to give it all up. Also if I'm world tennis champion I will have to travel!

My ideal job would be professional tennis player – that's just my dream. I think it's important to follow your dreams, even if you don't succeed. You just have to try.

How to get a job

Pour trouver un emploi, il faut d'abord poser sa candidature, en remplissant des fiches, avant d'assister à un entretien / interview.

To find a job, you have to apply by filling in forms before attending an interview.

Unemployment

Malheureusement, il y a un grand problème de chômage en Angleterre, surtout pour les jeunes qui viennent de terminer leurs études, et si on n'est pas suffisamment qualifié, on peut avoir du mal à trouver un boulot. J'ai horreur d'être au chômage à l'avenir. Les chômeurs risquent d'être atteints de la dépression et ne reçoivent que de ridicules allocations qui ne s'étendent même pas aux factures, et je ne parle même pas de vacances.

Unfortunately there is a big unemployment problem in England, especially for young people who have just finished school, and if you're not sufficiently qualified you can struggle to find a job. I am terrified of being unemployed in the future. The unemployed are at risk of depression and only get very small benefits which don't even cover the bills, not to mention holidays.

NOTES

HOUSE, HOME AND DAILY ROUTINES

Describe your house
J'habite une grande maison avec un jardin à l'arrière. Elle est ancienne et jolie, avec cinq chambres et deux salles de bain. J'aime ma maison parce que c'est confortable et il y a tout ce dont j'ai besoin, je ne suis pas obligé de partager ma chambre et ce n'est pas loin de mon école.

I live in a big house with a garden at the back. It's old and beautiful, with 5 bedrooms and two bathrooms. I like my house because it's comfortable and there is everything I need, I don't have to share a bedroom and it's not far from my school.

Describe your bedroom
Ma chambre est assez grande avec des murs bleus. Devant la porte se trouve mon lit et à côté il y a mon armoire et une étagère. J'aime ma chambre parce qu'il y a tout ce dont j'ai besoin, c'est confortable et bleu est ma couleur préférée.

My bedroom is quite big with blue walls. In front of the door is my bed and next to it there is my wardrobe and a bookshelf. I like my room because there is everything I need, it's comfortable and blue is my favourite colour.

Ideal house
Ma maison idéale serait énorme avec deux grandes piscines et beaucoup de chambres pour que mes amis puissent m'y rendre visite. Aussi, il y aurait un spa et un gymnase pour que je puisse rester en forme et un court de tennis ou je pourrais m'entrainer. Il y aurait un grand jardin avec beaucoup de fleurs et des arbres. Il faut que ce soit situé dans une ville animée comme Londres.

My ideal house would be enormous with two big swimming pools and lots of bedrooms so my friends could come and visit me. Also there would be a spa and a gym so I could keep fit and a tennis court where I could train. There would be a big garden with lots of flowers and trees. I would have to be situated in a lively town like London.

About you

Je m'appelle ………… et j'ai …. ans. Je suis de taille moyenne, j'ai les cheveux blonds et les yeux bleus. Je suis très marrant, sportif et assez intelligent mais parfois un peu paresseux, surtout le matin quand je n'ai pas envie d'aller au collège.

My name is ………. and I'm ….. years old. I am medium height, I have blond hair and blue eyes. I am very funny, sporty, and quite intelligent but sometimes a bit lazy, especially in the mornings when I don't want to go to school.

Describe your family

Il y a quatre personnes dans ma famille – mon père, ma mère, ma sœur et moi. Normalement on s'entend bien mais de temps en temps on se dispute. Ma sœur s'appelle Emily et elle a quatorze ans. Elle a les cheveux longs et blonds et les yeux marron. Elle est moins sportive que moi, elle est têtue et casse-pieds mais au moins on n'est pas obligé de partager une chambre. Ma mère est gentille et plus timide que mon père, qui n'arrête pas de faire l'andouille. J'en ai ras le bol !

There are 4 people in my family, my father, my mother, my two sisters and me. Normally we get on well but from time to time we argue. My sister is called Emily and she is 14. She has long blond hair and brown eyes. She is less sporty than me, she's stubborn and annoying but at least we don't have to share a room. My mother is kind and more introverted than my father who is always messing about. I've had enough of it!

The Ideal family / importance of marriage

Je ne pense pas qu'il y ait une famille idéale. Il y a toutes sortes de familles dans le monde, y compris les familles recomposées et monoparentales. L'important c'est que la famille passe du temps ensemble et que les enfants grandissent avec de la confiance et l'amour. J'ai de la chance parce que je trouve que ma famille est presqu'idéale.

I don't think there is such a thing as an ideal family. There are all sorts of families in the world including merged families and one parent families. The important thing is that the family spends time together and that the children grow up with confidence and love. I'm lucky because I think my family is almost ideal.

Describe your best friend - positive

Mon meilleur ami s'appelle James et il a les cheveux bruns et les yeux marron. Il est sportif et marrant et il me fait rire tout le temps. Ce que j'aime c'est que nous avons beaucoup de choses en commun, et il est toujours là pour moi. Cependant, quand j'ai envie d'être seul ça ne lui dérange pas. Nous avons tous les deux beaucoup de copains et on ne dépend pas l'un de l'autre.

My best friend is called James and he has brown hair and brown eyes. He is sporty and funny and he makes me laugh all the time. What I like is that we have lots of things in common and he is always there for me. However, when I feel like being on my own that doesn't bother him. We both have lots of friends and we don't depend on each other.

Best friend – future outings

Ce weekend on ira au cinéma avec des autres amis pour voir le nouveau film de Star Wars. J'ai hâte de le voir car j'ai entendu qu'il y a de bons effets spéciaux. Cette année il viendra en Espagne avec nous. Ce sera parfait.

This weekend we are going to go to the cinema with some other friends to see the new Star Wars film. I'm looking forward to seeing it because I have heard that there are good special effects. This year he is coming to Spain with us. It will be perfect.

Daily routine - week
Normalement pendant la semaine je me lève à sept heures, je me douche, je prends mon petit déjeuner et je quitte la maison à huit heures. J'arrive au collège à huit heures et demie, et je rentre à quatre heures. Chez moi, le soir, je fais mes devoirs, je prends mon diner en regardant la télé et je me couche vers dix heures.

Normally during the week I get up at 7, I shower, have breakfast and leave the house at 8. I arrive at school at 8.30 and I come home at 4. At home in the evening I do my homework, have my dinner watching TV and go to bed around 10.

Daily routine – weekend
Normalement le week-end je me lève plus tard que normalement, je me douche et je me brosse les dents. Je prends mon petit déjeuner et je quitte la maison à neuf heures pour aller à mon club de tennis. Je rentre chez moi à midi, et après avoir mangé je fais mes devoirs. Normalement je sors avec mes amis, au cinéma ou au parc, et puis je prends mon diner en regardant la télé. Puis je télécharge de la musique, ou bien je mets à jour mon profil Facebook et je bavarde sur le web avec mes copains. Je me couche vers dix heures mais souvent j'ai du mal à m'endormir donc je lis mon livre avant d'éteindre la lumière.

Normally at the weekend I get up later than usual, I shower and brush my teeth. I have breakfast and I leave the house at 9 to go to my tennis club. I come home at 12 and after eating I do my homework. Normally I go out with my friends to the cinema or the park and then I have my dinner watching TV. Then I download music or update my Facebook profile and I chat online with my friends. I go to bed around 10 but often I find it hard to go to sleep so I read my book before turning the light off.

This morning
Ce matin je me suis levé à six heures parce que je devais préparer mon examen oral de français. Je me suis douché et j'ai pris mon petit déjeuner avant de quitter la maison. Je suis arrivé au collège à huit heures et demie et j'ai bavardé avec mes copains.

This morning I got up at 6 because I had to revise for my French oral exam. I showered and had breakfast before leaving the house. I arrived at school at 8.30 and I chatted with my friends.

This evening
Ce soir je vais me détendre, car demain je n'aurai pas d'examens. Je vais regarder la télé et prendre mon diner avec mes parents. Ils vont m'interroger sur mon examen et je ne leur en dirai rien du tout !

Tonight I'm going to relax as I won't have any exams tomorrow. I am going to watch TV and have dinner with my parents. They will ask me all about my exam and I won't tell them anything at all.

What you would change about your routine
Si je pouvais changer quelque chose, je voudrais me lever plus tard et commencer l'école à midi, car je suis toujours fatigué le matin, et les scientifiques ont prouvé que les ados ont besoin de plus de sommeil le matin.

If I could change something I would like to get up later and start school at midday as I'm always tired in the mornings, and the scientists have proved that teenagers need more sleep in the morning.

Helping at home
Pour aider à la maison je range ma chambre de temps en temps, je fais la vaisselle et je mets la table, mais je ne fais pas beaucoup

parce que normalement j'ai trop de devoirs. Je pense que c'est important d'aider avec le ménage mais les devoirs sont plus importants, surtout juste avant les examens.

To help at home I tidy my room sometimes, I do the washing up and I lay the table but I don't do much because normally I have too much homework. I think it's important to help with housework but homework is more important, especially just before the exams.

Help at home yesterday
Hier j'ai mis la table pour donner un coup de main à ma mère, mais rien de plus car j'ai dû préparer mon examen de français.

Yesterday I laid the table and nothing else as I had to prepare for my French exam.

Cooking at home
Normalement c'est ma mère qui fait la cuisine. Elle prépare le diner pendant que je suis au collège, mais parfois si elle n'est pas là je prépare quelque chose comme les pâtes. Aussi j'adore faire des gâteaux parce que j'aime les manger !

Normally my mother does the cooking. She makes the dinner while I'm at school, but sometimes if she's not there I make something like pasta. Also I love making cakes because I like eating them.

Plans for next weekend with family
Le week-end prochain j'ai envie d'aller au cinéma pour voir le nouveau film qui s'appelle ………….. Ma mère a envie de le voir aussi. Après ça nous irons chez Starbucks pour prendre un chocolat chaud. Puis je rentrerai chez moi pour que je puisse manger avant d'aller à mon club de tennis pour m'entrainer pour mon prochain concours. Le soir je vais manger des pâtes et de la glace parce que j'aurai une faim de loup.

Next weekend I want to go to the cinema to see the new film called Bridge of Spies. My mother wants to see it as well. After that we will go to Starbucks for a hot chocolate. Then I will go back home so I can eat before going to my tennis club to train for my next competition. In the evening I am going to eat pasta and ice cream because I will be ravenous.

Last weekend with your family

Le weekend dernier nous sommes allés au parc pour promener le chien / jouer au foot, puis nous avions faim, donc nous sommes allés au restaurant près de chez moi et nous avons pris le déjeuner en bavardant. Après avoir mangé nous sommes rentrés et nous avons regardé un film ensemble. Ça fait du bien de passer du temps avec ma famille car on s'entend très bien et on s'amuse ensemble.

Last weekend we went to the park to walk the dog / play football, then we were hungry so we went to a restaurant near my house and had lunch while chatting. After eating we went home and watched a film together. It feels good to spend time with my family as we get on very well and we have fun together.

What you eat for breakfast

Au petit déjeuner je ne prends que des céréales et du jus d'orange car je n'ai jamais faim le matin.

For breakfast I only have cereal and orange juice as I am never hungry in the morning.

General eating habits

En général je mange sainement pour rester en forme parce que je suis sportif, mais mon repas préféré c'est la pizza car c'est délicieux et facile à préparer, suivi par de la glace au chocolat. Bien que ce soit malsain, c'est le meilleur repas du monde.

In general I eat healthily to stay fit because I'm sporty, but my favourite meal is pizza because it's delicious and easy to make, followed by chocolate icecream. Although it's unhealthy it's the best meal in the world.

What don't you like eating ?

Il n'y a rien que je n'aime pas manger mais je n'aime pas tellement les champignons.

There is nothing I don't like eating but I don't like mushrooms much.

Lunch at school

Je prends mon diner à la cantine au collège et pour la plupart c'est assez bon, mais de temps en temps les légumes sont trop cuits. Hier j'ai mangé du poulet avec des frites et des petits pois. C'était délicieux. Le soir j'ai mangé une omelette au fromage.

I have lunch in the school cantine and for the most part it's quite good but sometimes the vegetables are overcooked. Yesterday I ate chicken with chips and peas. It was delicious. In the evening I ate a cheese omelette.

Favourite food

J'adore la cuisine Italienne parce que je la trouve délicieuse et nous allons assez souvent à mon restaurant préféré parce que la pizza est à tomber. La dernière fois que j'y suis allé, j'ai autant mangé que je n'ai presque pas pu me lever de la table. J'ai eu les yeux plus gros que le ventre.

I love Italian food because I find it delicious and we quite often go to my favourite restaurant because the pizza is to die for. Last time I went there I at so much I could hardly get up from the table. My eyes were bigger than my stomach

How to stay healthy

Pour rester en forme il faut manger plein de légumes et de fruits, il faut boire huit verres d'eau par jour et éviter le sucre et la matière grasse, et bien sur l'alcool et le tabac. Il faut faire de l'exercice et passer du temps en plein air.

To stay healthy you have to eat lots of vegetables and fruit, you have to drink 8 glasses of water a day and avoid sugar and fat, and of course alcohol and tobacco. You should do exercise and spend time in the fresh air.

How you stay healthy

Pour moi c'est important de rester en forme car je joue au tennis plusieurs fois par semaine. J'y joue depuis cinq ans, j'y suis accro et je ne pourrais pas m'en passer. C'est le meilleur sport du monde. Donc pour la plupart je mange sainement et j'essaie d'éviter le sucre et la matière grasse, mais ce n'est pas toujours facile car j'adore le chocolat. En plus je bois un litre d'eau par jour, je dors huit heures par nuit et je m'entraine au gymnase tous les jours pour que je puisse gagner tous mes matchs de tennis. Je n'ai jamais fumé et je n'aime pas l'alcool. Peut-être que ça changera à l'avenir mais j'ai de bonnes intentions !

It's important to me to keep fit as I play tennis several times a week. I've been playing for 5 years, I am addicted to it and I couldn't manage without it. It's the best sport in the world. So for the most part I eat healthily and I try to avoid sugar and fat but it's not always easy as I love chocolate. I also drink a litre of water a day, I sleep 8 hours a night and I train at the gym every day so I can win all my tennis matches. I have never smoked and I don't like alcohol. Maybe that will change in the future but I have good intentions!

NOTES

Climate change

Le climat est en train de changer, il n'y a aucun doute. Il ne neige plus en hiver, tandis que pendant les années quatre-vingt il neigeait souvent. Le réchauffement de la terre a déjà causé l'augmentation du niveau des océans et il y a des iles qui commencent à disparaitre. En plus il y a de plus en plus d'ouragans et de tempêtes. Je trouve tout ça effrayant, car il me semble que c'est en cherchant une meilleure vie que nous détruisons notre planète.

There is no doubt that climate change is happening. It doesn't snow anymore in winter, whereas in the 80s it snowed a lot. Global warming has already caused ocean levels to rise and some islands are disappearing. Also there are more and more hurricanes and storms. I find all that frightening, as it seems to me that it is in searching for a better life that we are destroying our planet.

Climate change solution

Il faut qu'on fasse des efforts pour changer nos habitudes, consommer moins, voyager moins, gaspiller moins d'énergie et utiliser l'énergie renouvelable comme l'énergie solaire et éolienne. On devrait utiliser les transports en commun, recycler plus et construire plus de pistes cyclables pour encourager les gens à abandonner leurs voitures.

We've got to make an effort to change our habits, consume less, travel less, waste less energy and use renewable energy like solar and wind power. We should be using public transport, doing more recycling and building more cycle paths to encourage people to leave their cars at home.

Recycling

En famille on recycle tout ce qu'on peut – le verre, le plastique, le papier et le carton, et on va à la déchetterie pour recycler les choses plus grandes comme les meubles dont on n'a plus besoin.

In my family we recycle everything we can – glass, plastic, paper and cardboard,, and we go to the tip to recycle bigger things like furniture which we don't need anymore.

Importance of recycling

C'est important de recycler pour économiser nos ressources naturelles et parce qu'il n'y aura bientôt plus de place dans les décharges pour tous nos déchets.

It's important to recycle to conserve our natural resources and because soon there won't be any more space in landfill for all our rubbish.

What you do for the environment personally

Je fais beaucoup pour protéger l'environnement. Je prends une douche au lieu d'un bain pour économiser l'eau, j'éteins la lumière quand je quitte une pièce pour économiser l'électricité, je recycle les emballages comme le carton, le papier, le verre et le plastique, j'utilise le transport en commun et j'achète des produits écologiques.

I do a lot to protect the environment. I shower instead of having a bath to save water, I switch off the light when I leave a room to save electricity, I recycle packaging like cardboard, paper, glass and plastic, I use public transport and I buy green products.

What you do for the environment at school

Au collège, tout le monde fait beaucoup d'efforts pour protéger l'environnement. On a des poubelles de recyclage dans toutes les salles de classe, on éteint les lumières quand on sort d'une pièce, et on encourage les élèves à prendre le bus au lieu de la voiture pour aller au collège.

At school everyone makes a big effort to protect the environment. We have recycling bins in all the classrooms, we turn off the lights when we leave a room and the pupils are encouraged to use public transport instead of the car to travel to school.

What's the biggest problem in the world and what causes it ?

Je pense que la pollution atmosphérique, c'est le problème le plus grave auquel on fait face en ce moment. Ce qui cause la pollution, c'est d'abord les embouteillages et la circulation. Le problème c'est que les émissions des voitures causent la pollution de l'air, l'effet de serre, le réchauffement de la terre. J'en ai marre, et j'ai peur que quand je serai adulte ce sera difficile de respirer dans les grandes villes.

I think air pollution is the most serious problem we are facing at the moment. What causes pollution is firstly traffic jams and traffic. The problem is that the car emissions cause the air pollution, the greenhouse effect and global warming. I'm sick of it and I'm afraid that when I'm older it will be difficult to breathe in the big cities.

Why protect the environment ?

Si on ne protège pas la planète, il n'y aura bientôt plus de ressources naturelles, le trou dans la couche d'ozone grandira, et la race humaine disparaitra. Il faut qu'on fasse des efforts pour éviter cet avenir.

If we don't protect the planet, soon we will run out of natural resources, the hole in the ozone layer will get bigger and the human race will disappear. We need to make an effort to avoid this outcome.

What should we be doing for the environment ?
On devrait utiliser les transports en commun au lieu de la voiture, construire plus de pistes cyclables, voyager moins en avion et acheter des produits fabriqués dans notre pays.

We should use public transport instead of the car, build more cycle paths, travel less by plane and buy products made in our country.

Do you watch TV?
Je ne regarde jamais la télé parce que les profs nous donnent trop de devoirs donc je n'ai pas le temps, mais j'écoute la radio parfois en faisant mes devoirs. Si jamais j'ai du temps libre, je préfère regarder un film sur Netflix.

I never watch TV because the teachers give us too much homework so I don't have the time, but I listen to the radio sometimes while doing my homework. If every I have free time I prefer to watch a film on Netflix.

Young people and TV

C'est vrai que les jeunes regardent beaucoup de télé, mais je pense que le problème est plutôt qu'ils passent trop de temps devant les écrans à jouer aux jeux-vidéo. Ce serait mieux de regarder la télé, parce que là au moins il y a des émissions éducatives, les infos, des documentaires etcetera.

It's true that young people watch a lot of TV but I think that the problem is more that they spend too much time in front of screens playing video games. It would be better to watch TV because there at least there are educational programmes, news, documentaries etc.

Importance of news

Les infos sont importantes parce qu'il faut qu'on sache ce qu'il se passe dans le monde pour avoir une opinion là-dessus et pour pouvoir réagir de manière appropriée. Si on n'est pas suffisamment informé, on peut être berné par les medias.

News is important because we need to know what's going on in the world in order to have an opinion on it and in order to be able to react appropriately. If you're not well-informed enough you can get brainwashed by the media.

What's in the news at the moment ?

Actuellement c'est le climat qui fait la une - il y a des inondations partout et des centaines de maisons ont été détruites. En plus il y a les attentats terroristes en France et aux Etats Unis, que je trouve de plus en plus inquiétants.

Right now it's climate that's making the headlines – there are floods everywhere and hundreds of houses have been destroyed. Also there are the terrorist attacks in France and in the USA which I find more and more worrying.

Do you read a paper ?

Je ne lis pas le journal, parce que je trouve que c'est plus vite en ligne et j'ai l'application de la BBC sur mon portable qui me prévient chaque fois qu'il y a quelque chose d'important à savoir.

I don't read the paper because I find it's faster online and I have the BBC app on my phone which notifies me every time there's something important to know.

Which is the most popular newspaper ?

Je pense que les journaux les plus populaires ce sont les journaux de petit format, les journaux à sensation. Ils ne contiennent rien d'intéressant, et ils ne servent qu'à faire peur aux gens en leur disant par exemple que notre pays sera bientôt envahi par les musulmans, que le gouvernement est nul, que tout est un désastre. Je déteste ces journaux.

I think that the most popular newspapers are the sensationalist tabloids. They don't have anything interesting in them and all they do is frighten people by saying for example that our country is about to be invaded by Muslims, that the government is no good, that everything is a disaster. I hate those newspapers.

Importance of advertising

Je trouve la publicité nécessaire pour l'économie, car les entreprises en ont besoin pour se faire connaitre. Cependant, la pub pour la malbouffe devrait être interdite comme la pub pour les cigarettes, car elles sont tellement mauvaises pour la santé.

I think that advertising is necessary for the economy as companies need it to make themselves known. However, advertising junk food should be banned like advertising cigarettes as they are so bad for the health.

Cinema or TV ?

Je préfère le cinéma parce que c'est plus passionnant que rester dans le salon. J'aime les films d'action parce qu'il y a de bons effets spéciaux. Cependant, les billets coutent les yeux de la tête et je n'ai pas les moyens d'y aller plus qu'une fois par mois.

I prefer the cinema because it's more exciting that staying in the living room. I like action films because there are good special effects. However, the tickets cost the earth and I can't afford to go more than once a month.

Mobile phones – do you have one and why ?

Oui, j'ai un portable dont je me sers tous les jours – pour rester en contact avec mes parents, mes amis, pour envoyer des textos et pour mettre à jour mon statut sur Facebook. Je ne pourrais pas m'en passer, j'y suis tout à fait accro.

Yes I have a mobile that I use every day – to stay in touch with my parents, my friends, to send texts and to update my Facebook status. I couldn't do without it, I'm completely addicted to it.

Young people and mobile phones

Les jeunes aiment les portables parce qu'ils sont tellement utiles, pour rester en contact avec ses amis, pour envoyer les textos et pour surfer le web, écouter de la musique, prendre des photos et jouer aux jeux sur les applications.

Young people like mobile phones because they are so useful, to stay in touch with friends, to send texts and use the internet, to listen to music, take photos and play games on apps.

Dangers of mobile phones

Le danger principal c'est qu'on peut perdre beaucoup de temps en faisant tout ça, et devenir accro au portable. Aussi, si on traverse la rue en regardant son portable on pourrait facilement avoir un accident. De plus il y a le risque de vol d'identité et de cyber intimidation sur les réseaux sociaux.

The main danger is that you can waste a lot of time doing all that, and become addicted to the phone. Also if you cross the road looking at your phone you could easily have an accident. There is also the risk of identity theft and online bullying on social networks.

The future of mobile phones

A l'avenir, les portables vont devenir encore plus légers, encore plus utiles, encore plus puissants. Mais exactement comment ? J'ai du mal à m'imaginer.

In the future, mobile phones will become even lighter, even more useful, even more powerful. But how exactly? I find it hard to imagine.

Importance of computers / internet

L'ordinateur c'est indispensable pour moi et je pense qu'à l'avenir ils seront de plus en plus importants pour tout le monde. On ne pourra pas travailler sans ordinateur. Je l'ai utilisé hier soir pour faire mes devoirs et pour envoyer des emails. Le plus grand avantage de l'ordinateur c'est que c'est le meilleur moyen de surfer le web et d'accéder à l'internet. Avec internet on peut communiquer avec les gens à l'étranger face à face sur Skype, on peut télécharger des films et de la musique, on peut envoyer des messages et faire du commerce.

The computer is essential to me and I think that in the future they will be more and more important for everyone. We won't be able to work without a computer. I used it last night to do my homework and to send emails. The biggest advantage of the computer is that it's the best way of surfing the web and going on the internet. With the internet you can communicate with people abroad face to face on Skype, you can download films and music, you can send messages and do business.

Disadvantages of computers / internet

L'inconvénient c'est que l'internet présente des dangers pour tout le monde. Le danger principal c'est qu'on peut perdre beaucoup de temps en faisant tout ça, et devenir accro au portable. Aussi, si on traverse la rue en regardant son portable on pourrait facilement avoir un accident. De plus il y a le risque de vol d'identité et de cyber intimidation sur les réseaux sociaux. Il y a des enfants qui ont été tués par les inconnus qu'ils ont rencontrés en ligne. Et bien que les personnes âgées qui vivent seules, puissent maintenant avoir les moyens de rester en contact avec le monde, la plupart de ces personnes n'ont pas toujours envie d'apprendre comment en profiter car ils le trouvent trop compliqué.

The disadvantage is that the internet presents dangers for everyone. The main danger is that you can waste a lot of time doing all that, and become addicted to the phone. Also if you cross the road looking at your phone you could easily have an accident. There is also the risk of identity theft and online bullying on social networks. There are children who have been killed by strangers they have met online. And although old people living alone can now have the means to stay in contact with the world, most of these people don't always want to learn to make the most of it as they find it too complicated.

NOTES

SOCIAL ACTIVITIES, FITNESS AND HEALTH

Your birthday

Mon anniversaire est le neuf mai

My birthday is the 9th of May

Importance of your birthday

J'adore mon anniversaire. C'est la date la plus importante de l'année car je reçois plein de cadeaux et mes parents font tout pour que je puisse me détendre et faire tout ce que je veux.

I love my birthday. It's the most important date of the year as I receive lots of presents and my parents do everything so I can relax and do everything I want.

Your last birthday

Pour fêter mon dernier anniversaire, je suis allé au restaurant avec ma famille et j'ai mangé mon repas préféré, la pizza. C'était super et je me suis bien amusée. Cependant après avoir mangé je suis rentrée chez moi et, quelle désastre – le chien avait mangé mon gâteau d'anniversaire ! On a dû aller en chercher un autre au magasin.

To celebrate my last birthday I went to the restaurant with my family and I ate my favourite meal, pizza. It was great and I had a lot of fun. However, after eating, I went home and, what a disaster, the dog had eaten my birthday cake. We had to go and get another one from the shop.

How will you celebrate the end of exams ?

Pour fêter la fin des examens j'irai chez Nandos avec tous mes amis, et après avoir mangé je vais rentrer chez moi et dormir quinze heures.

To celebrate the end of the exams I will go to Nandos with all my friends and after eating I will go home and sleep for 15 hours.

How to stay healthy

Pour rester en forme il faut manger plein de légumes et de fruits, il faut boire huit verres d'eau par jour et il faut éviter le sucre et la matière grasse, et bien sur l'alcool et le tabac. Il faut faire de l'exercice et passer du temps en plein air.

To stay healthy you have to eat lots of vegetables and fruit, you have to drink 8 glasses of water a day and avoid sugar and fat, and of course alcohol and tobacco. You should do exercise and spend time in the fresh air.

How you stay healthy

Pour moi c'est important de rester en forme car je joue au tennis plusieurs fois par semaine. J'y joue depuis cinq ans, j'y suis accro et je ne pourrais pas m'en passer. C'est le meilleur sport du monde. Donc pour la plupart je mange sainement et j'essaie d'éviter le sucre et la matière grasse, mais ce n'est pas toujours facile car j'adore le chocolat. En plus je bois un litre d'eau par jour, je dors huit heures par nuit et je m'entraine au gymnase tous les jours pour que je puisse gagner tous mes matchs de tennis. Je n'ai jamais fumé et je n'aime pas l'alcool. Peut-être que ça changera à l'avenir mais j'ai de bonnes intentions !

It's important to me to keep fit as I play tennis several times a week. I've been playing for 5 years, I am addicted to it and I couldn't manage without it. It's the best sport in the world. So for the most part I eat healthily and I try to avoid sugar and fat but it's not always easy as I love chocolate. I also drink a litre of water a day, I sleep 8 hours a night and I train at the gym every day so I can win all my tennis matches. I have never smoked and I don't like alcohol. Maybe that will change in the future but I have good intentions!

Sickness

J'ai de la chance parce que je ne tombe malade que très rarement. Normalement si ce n'est pas grave, il faut rester au lit mais si tu ne vas pas mieux après quelques jours il faut aller chez le médecin, qui te donnera des médicaments ou des comprimes.

I'm lucky because I only very rarely get ill. Normally if it's not serious you have to stay in bed but if you're not better after a few days you have to go to the doctor who will give you medicine or pills.

Smoking

Pour moi, fumer c'est ridicule, car on sait que ça raccourcit la vie et ça entraine de graves maladies comme le cancer. Je ne fumerai jamais. Je pense que les ados commencent à fumer pour de diverses raisons. La raison principale c'est la pression du groupe. Si on va à une soirée il y a toujours des ados qui fument sans que leurs parents ne le sachent et il y aura toujours des autres qui veulent faire partie du groupe, mais pas moi non.

For me, smoking is ridiculous as we know it shortens your life and causes serious illnesses like cancer. I will never smoke. I think young people start smoking for a variety of reasons. The main reason is peer pressure. If you go to a party there are always teenagers smoking without their parents' knowledge and there will always be others who want to be part of the group, but not me.

Alcohol

Pour moi, l'alcool c'est ridicule, car on sait que ça raccourcit la vie et ça entraine de graves maladies comme le cancer et les crises cardiaques. Je ne boirai jamais. Je pense que les ados commencent à boire pour de diverses raisons. La raison principale c'est la pression du groupe. Si on va à une soirée il y a toujours des ados qui boivent sans que leurs parents ne le sachent et il y aura toujours des autres qui veulent faire partie du groupe, mais pas moi non.

For me, alcohol is ridiculous as we know it shortens your life and causes serious illnesses like cancer and heart attacks. I will never drink. I think young people start drinking for a variety of reasons. The main reason is peer pressure. If you go to a party there are always teenagers drinking without their parents' knowledge and there will always be others who want to be part of the group, but not me.

Drugs

Pour moi, les drogues sont ridicules, car on sait que ça raccourcit la vie et ça entraine de graves maladies comme le cancer. Je n'en prendrai jamais. Je pense que les ados commencent à se droguer pour de diverses raisons. La raison principale c'est la pression du groupe. Si on va à une soirée il y a toujours des ados qui se droguent sans que leurs parents ne le sachent et il y aura toujours des autres qui veulent faire partie du groupe, mais pas moi non.

For me, drugs are ridiculous as we know it shortens your life and causes serious illnesses like cancer. I will never take any. I think young people start taking drugs for a variety of reasons. The main reason is peer pressure. If you go to a party there are always teenagers taking drugs without their parents' knowledge and there will always be others who want to be part of the group, but not me.

Vegetarianism

Je pense que les gens deviennent végétariens pour de diverses raisons. Normalement c'est parce qu'ils ne veulent pas tuer les animaux, mais il y a des gens qui le font pour des raisons de santé, ou bien pour des raisons environnementales. On dit que si on arrêtait de détruire les forêts tropicales en sud-Amérique pour y mettre des vaches, la planète aurait plus de chance de survivre. Le bœuf n'est pas aussi important qu'il faille sacrifier notre monde.

I think that people become vegetarian for a variety of reasons. Normally it's because they don't want to kill animals, but there are people who do it for reasons of health or for environmental reasons. They say that if we stopped destroying the tropical forests in South America to graze cows, the planet would have a better chance of surviving. Beef is not so important that we have to sacrifice our world.

Sport and hobbies

Je suis accro au sport parce que c'est amusant, énergique et bon pour la santé. Je joue au tennis deux fois par semaine. J'ai de la chance parce que je suis membre d'un club de tennis depuis cinq ans et je fais partie de l'équipe scolaire. En plus je joue au foot et au rugby et je fais de l'athlétisme. Pendant les vacances je fais du vélo avec mon père.

I'm addicted to sport because it's fun, energetic and good for your health. I play tennis twice a week. I'm lucky because I have been a member of a tennis club for five years and I am in my school team. I also play football and rugby and I do athletics. During the holidays I go cycling with my father.

Hobbies when you were young
Quand j'étais jeune je faisais moins de sport mais je passais la plupart de mon temps à jouer dans le parc avec mes amis. En plus, je regardais la télévision et je jouais aux jeux de société avec ma famille.

When I was young I did less sport but I spent most of my time playing in the park with my friends. I also used to watch TV and play board games with my family.

Ideal weekend

Mon week-end idéal serait chez moi avec ma famille et mes amis. Je jouerais au foot dans le jardin, j'irais au cinéma pour voir un film d'action et je mangerais dans un bon restaurant. Le lendemain j'irais à la piscine pour faire de la natation et après être rentre chez moi je regarderais un film sur Netflix, en mangeant des bonbons.

My ideal weekend would be at home with my family and friends. I would play football in the garden, I'd go to the cinema to see an action film and I'd eat in a good restaurant. The next day I'd go to the pool to swim and after coming home I would watch a film on Netflix while eating sweets.

Books you've read

Je lis des livres de temps en temps mais pas assez souvent. Je suis en train de lire 'Child 44 ». Il s'agit d'un garçon en Russie qui grandit en pauvreté mais qui commence à travailler pour le KGB. C'est super-passionnant. Le suspense m'a tenu en haleine jusqu'à la fin.

I read books from time to time but not often enough. I'm in the middle of reading Child 44. It's about a boy in Russia who grows up in poverty but who starts working for the KGB. It's very exciting. I was on the edge of my seat right to the end.

Do you watch TV?

Je ne regarde jamais la télé parce que les profs nous donnent trop de devoirs donc je n'ai pas le temps, mais j'écoute la radio parfois en faisant mes devoirs. Si jamais j'ai du temps libre, je préfère regarder un film sur Netflix.

I never watch TV because the teachers give us too much homework so I don't have the time, but I listen to the radio sometimes while doing my homework. If every I have free time I prefer to watch a film on Netflix.

Young people and TV

C'est vrai que les jeunes regardent beaucoup de télé, mais je pense que le problème est plutôt qu'ils passent trop de temps devant les écrans à jouer aux jeux-vidéo. Ce serait mieux de regarder la télé, parce que là au moins il y a des émissions éducatives, les infos, des documentaires etcetera.

It's true that young people watch a lot of TV but I think that the problem is more that they spend too much time in front of screens playing video games. It would be better to watch TV because there at least there are educational programmes, news, documentaries etc.

Music and musicians

Je ne joue pas d'instrument mais j'aime la musique. Le style que je préfère c'est le rock, car c'est très fort et il y a beaucoup d'instruments, c'est énergique et ça me fait plaisir de l'écouter. J'ai envie de voir mon chanteur préféré, Ed Sheeran en concert mais il faut que je fasse des taches ménagères chez moi pour gagner l'argent pour payer l'entrée. C'est comme ça que ça marche chez moi. J'aime Ed Sheeran parce qu'il est tellement doué et sa voix me donne un frisson quand je l'écoute. Il m'a inspiré parce qu'il vient d'une famille pauvre et il a travaillé toute sa vie pour réussir.

I don't play an instrument but I like music. The type I prefer is rock as it's very loud and there are lots of instruments, it's energetic and it makes me happy listening to it. I'd like to see my favourite singer Ed Sheeran in concert but I have to do housework to earn the money to buy the tickets. That's how it works at my house. I like Ed Sheeran because he's so talented and his voice gives me goose bumps when I listen to him. He has inspired me because he comes from a poor family and he worked all his life to succeed.

Your favourite type of TV programme

À mon avis, les feuilletons sont les meilleures émissions parce qu'elles sont captivantes et grisantes. Elles me font rire et pleurer. Si j'avais plus de temps libre j'en regarderais plus mais les profs nous donnent trop de devoirs.

In my opinion, soaps are the best programmes because they are exciting and intoxicating, they make me laugh and cry. If I had more free time I'd watch more of them but the teachers give us too much homework.

Your favourite type of film

Je dirais que je préfère les films d'action parce qu'il y a de bons effets spéciaux. Ils sont plus passionnants que les films romantiques et moins effrayants que les films d'horreur.

I would say that I prefer action films because there are good special effects. They are more exciting than romance films and less scary than horror films.

The last film you saw

Le dernier film que j'ai vu était la Mort de Stalin. C'était une comédie, mais je ne l'ai pas trouvé drôle, donc j'ai été un peu déçue. Cependant, j'ai appris quelque chose sur l'histoire de la Russie donc ça a valu la peine d'y aller. Les acteurs ont super-bien joué. J'ai préféré Maze Runner que j'ai vu l'année dernière. J'etais scotché à l'écran jusqu'au dernier moment du film.

The last film I saw was the Death of Stalin. It was a comedy but I didn't find it funny so I was a bit disappointed. However, I learnt something about the history of Russia so it was worth going. The actors played really well. I preferred Maze Runner which I saw last year. I was glued to the screen until the last moment of the film.

French films you have seen

J'ai vu un film français qui s'appelle 'Les Choristes', un film de Christophe Barratier. C'est l'histoire d'un prof de musique dans un internat de rééducation. En enseignant le chant choral, il réussit à transformer la vie des garçons. Je l'ai trouvé amusant et triste en même temps.

I saw a French film called "the choristers", a Christophe Barratier film. It's the story of a music teacher in a boarding school. By teaching choral singing he manages to transform the lives of the boys. I found it fun and sad at the same time

Cinema or TV ?

Je préfère le cinéma parce que c'est plus passionnant que rester dans le salon. J'aime les films d'action parce qu'il y a de bons effets spéciaux. Cependant, les billets coutent les yeux de la tête et je n'ai pas les moyens d'y aller plus qu'une fois par mois.

I prefer the cinema because it's more exciting that staying in the living room. I like action films because there are good special effects. However, the tickets cost the earth and I can't afford to go more than once a month.

The last book you read

Le dernier roman que j'ai lu était les jeux de faim. Il s'agit d'enfants qui doivent se battre dans un milieu dangereux dans un jeu télévisé. Les télé spectateur peuvent leur livrer des cadeaux pour les aider a survivre, et il n'y a qu'un seul gagnant. Tous les autres meurent.

The last book I read was the Hunger Games. It's about children who have to fight in a dangerous environment in a TV show. The TV audience can deliver them presents to help them survive and there is only one winner. All the others die.

Pocket money and shopping

Moi je déteste faire du shopping et je ne le fais jamais, sauf quand je suis obligé d'acheter de nouveaux vêtements parce que là, ma mère ne sait pas mon goût. Je reçois dix livres par semaine mais j'essaie d'économiser mon argent au lieu de le gaspiller. La dernière chose que j'ai achetée c'est les billets de cinéma pour Star Wars. Ça valait la peine. C'était excellent ! Quant aux courses, ma mère fait tout en ligne.

I hate shopping and I never do it, except when I have to buy new clothes because my mother doesn't know my taste. I receive ten pounds a week but I try to save my money instead of wasting it. The last thing I bought was cinema tickets for Star Wars. It was worth it. It was excellent! As for food shopping, my mother does it all on line.

PART 3

ROLE PLAY

NOTES

Role play at GCSE

The role play element does not exist yet in Edexcel IGCSE but is super-useful as an exercise if you want to feel confident out and about in a French-speaking country, some would say essential! Other exam boards give you a short time to prepare a role play exercise where you will usually play the role of a student going to stay with a family, or a tourist needing some information. Be prepared to talk about something going wrong, like leaving your bag in the restaurant, your wallet in the taxi, missing planes and losing passports.

The best way to prepare for this is to revise set phrases that often arise, so they are grouped below in subject matter.

Initiating a conversation

Excusez-moi	Excuse me
Je peux vous aider	Can I help you ?
Allo ?	Hello (answering phone)
Salut	Hi / Hey
Bonjour / Bonsoir	Hello (formal)
Je vous appelle parce que	I'm calling you because
J'ai réservé une chambre	I have reserved a room

Directions

Pour aller à la gare ?	How do I get to the station?
Allez tout droit	Go straight on
Jusqu'aux feux	Until the lights
Prenez	Take
La première rue à droite	the first road on the right
La deuxième rue à gauche	the second left

Apologizing

Je suis désolé	I'm sorry
Pardon	Excuse me (bumping into someone)

Lateness and reasons for lateness

Je suis en retard	I'm late
Je vais arriver	I'm going to arrive
Plus tard que j'avais prévu	later than I had planned
Le vol a été annule	the flight was cancelled
Je me suis dispute avec	I argued with
J'ai raté le train	I missed the train

Losing things

J'ai perdu mon passeport	I have lost my passport
J'ai laissé mon sac dans...	I left my bag in….
J'ai oublié mon portefeuille	I have forgotten my wallet

Asking questions

The rule is this : if you use a question word like ou, comment, quand, pourquoi, then you will need to either invert verb and subject (*pourquoi es-tu triste?*) or use est-ce que in between the question word and the statement (*pourquoi est-ce que tu es triste?*)

Où est la gare?	Where is the station ?
A quelle heure part le train ?	When does the train leave?
Qu'est-ce qu'on va faire ?	What are we going to do?
Qu'est-ce que tu aimes manger ?	What do you like eating?
Comment vas-tu ?	How are you ?
Comment vas-tu au collège ?	How do you get to school?

Comment est ta maison ?	What's your house like ?
Quand est-ce qu'on va partir ?	When are we leaving ?
Pourquoi es-tu triste ?	Why are you sad ?
Combien d'argent as-tu ?	How much money have you got?

However, if there is no question word involved (so no *how, when, where, who, which, how much, what*) then all you have to do is put the question as a statement with a question mark at the end:

Tu as un chien?	You have a dog? Do you have a dog?
Il fait beau?	Is the weather good?
Vous avez une table ?	Do you have a table?

Stating preferences

Je voudrais aller au cinéma	I'd like to go to the cinema
Je préfère nager	I prefer swimming
Je n'aime pas les champignons	I don't like mushrooms
J'adore le cinéma	I love the cinema

Understanding instructions in the role play

Whereas the AQA board role play relates closely to the material in the general conversation, Cambridge IGCSE requires the candidate to understand instructions such as

Réagissez avec plaisir	react with pleasure
Posez une question	ask a question
Répondez à la question	answer the question
Expliquez la situation	explain the situation
Saluez votre ami	say hello to your friend
Dites ce que vous faites	say what you're doing

Proposez de payer	offer to pay
Expliquez pourquoi	explain why
Demandez le prix	ask the price
Faites vos excuses	apologise
Choisissez un dessert	choose a pudding

The role play will include a surprise question. Have a look at the situation described and try to imagine what might come up. It will probably be an opportunity to say what you like or want to do, or a question about your family, friends, school or holiday. Remember you know all this from revision of the general conversation questions and answers.

PART 4

GLOSSARY OF IMPRESSIVE PHRASES

NOTES

VERB TENSES

Make sure you have used:

- Present (including irregulars and reflexives) to describe what you normally do
- Passé composé (using etre and avoir and reflexives) to describe events in the past
- Imperfect to describe repeated actions in the past or unfinished action
- Both types of future tense and future used with quand – *quand je serai adulte...*
- Conditional (including combining with imperfect in an *if* sentence)
- (possibly) pluperfect, in conjunction with passé compose to describe what *had* happened
- Past conditional, with pluperfect, to say what you would have done *if...*

SPECIAL VERB STRUCTURES

En lisant	while reading
Après avoir mangé	after eating
Avant de sortir	before going out
Je suis en train de	I'm in the middle of
Je viens de	I have just
Sur le point de	about to

OPINIONS AND JUSTIFICATIONS

Je pense que	I think that
Je trouve que	I find that
Je le trouve facile	I find it easy
A mon avis	In my opinion
Selon moi	according to me
Parce que / car c'est	because it is

POSITIVE OPINIONS ON THINGS

Ça vaut la peine	it's worth it
Ça valait la peine	it was worth it
Ça fait du bien	it feels good
Ça me fait plaisir	it makes me happy
Je suis ravi de partir en vacances	I'm excited about my holiday
J'ai hâte d'y retourner	I can't wait to go back there
J'attends ……. avec impatience	I am looking forward to ……
On a passé un bon moment	we had a great time
C'est à tomber	it's to die for
Ça me fait rire	it makes me laugh
Je suis fort en maths	I'm good at maths

NEGATIVE OPINIONS ON THINGS

J'en ai marre	I'm sick of it
J'en ai ras le bol	I've had enough
Ça me fait peur	I'm scared of it
C'est nul	It's rubbish
Je suis nul en maths	I'm rubbish at maths
J'ai horreur de	I have a horror of / hate
Un cauchemar	a nightmare

AVOIR EXPRESSIONS

J'ai de la chance	I'm lucky
J'ai envie de	I want to, I feel like
J'ai du mal à	I find it hard to
J'ai hâte de	I'm looking forward to / can't wait to
J'ai besoin de	I need
Tout ce dont j'ai besoin	everyting I need (of which I have need)

COMPARATIVES AND SUPERLATIVES

Plus sympa que	nicer than
Moins sportif que	less sporty than
Le film le plus passionnant	the most exciting film
Le meilleur pays du monde	the best country in the world

Y AND DEPUIS

J'y habite depuis cinq ans	I've lived there for five years
J'y joue depuis cinq ans	I've been playing it for five years
J'ai envie d'y retourner un jour	I'd like to go back there
J'y suis accro	I'm addicted to it
Je n'y suis jamais allé	I've never been there

EN

Je m'en sers pour tout	I use it for everything
J'en profite	I make the most of it
Je n'en prends jamais	I never take any (drugs)
J'en mange tous les jours	I eat it (some of it) evey day
Il n'y en a pas	there aren't any (cycle paths)
Il n'y en a pas assez	there aren't enough of them
Je ne pourrais pas m'en passer	I couldn't manage without it

DONT

Il y a tout ce dont j'ai besoin	there is everything I need
Tout ce dont j'ai besoin	everyting I need

PRECEDING DIRECT / INDIRECT OBJECTS

Les profs nous donnent	the teachers give us
Je le trouve ennuyeux	I find it boring
Ça ne lui dérange pas	it doesn't bother him
Je lui ai acheté un cadeau	I bought him / her a presesnt

SUBJUNCTIVE EXPRESSIONS

Pour que je puisse	so that I can
Bien que ce soit	although it is
Quoi que ce soit	whatever it may be
Il faut qu'on fasse des efforts pour	we've got to try to
Avant que ce ne soit trop tard	before it's too late
Je ne pense pas que ce soit	I don't think it is

Sans que leurs parents ne le sachent
without their parents' knowledge

POUR + INFINITIVE

pour regarder un film	to watch a film
pour acheter un cadeau	to buy a present

DE WITH ADJECTIVES THAT COME BEFORE THE NOUN

De bonnes notes	good marks
De mauvaises notes	bad marks
De bons effets spéciaux	good special effects
Pour de diverses raisons	for a variety of reasons

IMPERSONAL EXPRESSIONS

On peut	one can / you can
On doit	one must / you have to
Il faut	you have to
Il me faut (plus time)	it takes me
Il me faut (plus noun)	I need
Il suffit de	all you have to do is
Il s'agit de	it's about

MODALS IN ALL TENSES

On doit porter un uniforme	we have to wear uniform
J'ai dû en acheter un autre	I had to buy another
On devrait recycler plus	we should recycle more
J'aurais dû appeler	I should have called
Je ne pouvais pas m'en sortir	I couldn't manage
Il aurait pu faire des efforts	he could have made an effort
Je voudrais apprendre à nager	I would like to learn to swim
Je ne veux pas commencer à fumer	I don't want to start smoking

NEGATIVES

Je ne fume pas	I don't smoke
Je n'ai jamais fume	I have never smoked
Je ne le ferai plus	I won't do it anymore
Personne ne fume	Nobody smokes
Il n'y a aucune raison	There is no reason
Il n'y a rien à faire	There's nothing to do

Il n'y a que des anglais ici — there are only English people here

CE QUE

Ce que j'aime le plus c'est	what I like best is
Ce que je n'aime pas, c'est que	what I don't like is

IDIOMS

J'en ai marre	I'm sick of it
J'en ai ras le bol	I've had enough
Ils ont du mal à se débrouiller	they struggle to get by
Il fait un froid de canard	it's freezing cold
Il pleut des grenouilles	it's pouring
Je n'en ferai pas une rame	I won't lift a finger
Les billets coutent les yeux de la tête	the tickets cost a bomb
Donner un coup de main à qq	give someone a hand
Scotché à l'écran	glued to the screen
Le suspense m'a tenu en haleine	I was riveted
J'ai eu les yeux plus gros que le ventre	my eyes were bigger than my stomach
Il n'arrête pas de faire l'andouille	he doesn't stop messing about

NOTES

Other publications also available on Amazon:

How to Ace your French oral

How to Ace your Spanish oral

How to Ace your German oral

French vocabulary for GCSE

Spanish vocabulary for GCSE

The Common Entrance French Handbook

Brush up your French – a revision guide for grown-ups

The Advanced French Handbook

Ten Magic tricks with French

Spanish in a week

If you have any comments or questions on any of the content of this book, please do get in touch via my website

www.lucymartintuition.co.uk

Find me on Facebook and like my page to be first in the running for news and offers and free books!

And for some extra tips on how to impress examiners with your oral and writing, subscribe to my Lucy Martin Tuition YouTube channel.

Printed in Great Britain
by Amazon